Simone Cave was the health editor at the *Daily Mirror* for eight years and is now a freelance journalist covering health and medical issues for national newspapers and magazines. She lives with her husband and three children in South London. Simone can be contacted via: www.yourbabyandchild.com

Dr Caroline Fertleman is Consultant Paediatrician at the Whittington Hospital, London and also works at the Institute of Child Health (UCL) and has an honorary contract with Great Ormond Street Hospital. She lives in London with her husband and three children.

Potty Training Boys

... the easy way

Simone Cave and
Dr Caroline Fertleman

LONDON

7 9 10 8

Published in 2008 by Vermilion, an imprint of Ebury Publishing

Ebury Publishing is a Random House Group company

The Random House Group Limited Reg. No. 954009

Addresses for companies within the Random House Group can be found at
www.rbooks.co.uk

A CIP catalogue record for this book is available from the British Library

Mixed Sources
Product group from well-managed
forests and other controlled sources
www.fsc.org Cert no. TT-COC-2139
© 1996 Forest Stewardship Council
FSC

The Random House Group Limited supports The Forest Stewardship
Council (FSC), the leading international forest certification organisation.
All our titles that are printed on Greenpeace approved FSC certified paper
carry the FSC logo. Our paper procurement policy can be found at
www.rbooks.co.uk/environment

Printed and bound in Great Britain by
CPI Cox & Wyman, Reading, RG1 8EX

ISBN 9780091917340

Copies are available at special rates for bulk orders. Contact the
sales development team on 020 7840 8487 or visit
www.booksforpromotions.co.uk for more information.

To buy books by your favourite authors and register for offers, visit
www.rbooks.co.uk

The information in this book has been compiled by way of general
guidance in relation to the specific subjects addressed, but is not a
substitute and not to be relied on for medical, healthcare, pharmaceutical
or other professional advice on specific circumstances and in specific
locations. Please consult your GP before changing, stopping or starting
any medical treatment. So far as the authors are aware the information
given is correct and up to date as at December 2007. Practice, laws and
regulations all change, and the reader should obtain up-to-date
professional advice on any such issues. The authors and publishers
disclaim, as far as the law allows, any liability arising directly or indirectly
from the use, or misuse, of the information contained in this book.

CONTENTS

CONTENTS

We dedicate this book to Lewis, Douglas,
Harry and Tobias.

ACKNOWLEDGEMENTS

With thanks to:

Paul Johnson, Judy Cave, Barbara Levy, Julia Kellaway, Adrian Cohen, Jo Carroll and assorted paediatricians at the Whittington Hospital.

Introduction

I f you've got a little boy then you've probably discovered that he's been dealt an extra dose of energy and lacks some of the common sense that little girls seem to be born with.

So when it comes to potty training, it's no surprise that it can be more challenging to teach boys than girls – boys are known to take longer, learn later and to have more problems than girls. On average, most boys aren't physically ready to be potty trained until they are about two and a half; with girls it's generally a few months earlier.

We've written *Potty Training Boys* to help guide you and your son gently through the stages of leaving nappies behind so he is able to go to the toilet alone, even at night. By following our training programme it should take a couple of weeks for your son to become nappy-free at home, but a bit longer for night training and to leave the house without nappies.

Although we've written *Potty Training Boys* with mums in mind; dads, grandparents and any other carers can obviously use this book too. We particularly encourage dads to take the main role in potty training their sons because being male is a real advantage to teaching little boys.

SIMPLE, STRESS-FREE POTTY TRAINING

Our fundamental aim has been to get into the heads of little boys so that even the most wilful or boisterous child will happily relinquish his nappies and start using the potty and toilet without any hang-ups. We've ensured that the potty-training process will be simple and painless for both parents and their sons.

Unlike the more intensive methods that some people opt for, our more laid-back approach is, we feel, much better suited to boys. Using our techniques, there's no need to take a week off work or to carry a potty in the buggy 'just in case'.

You'll find this potty-training programme stress-free with very few accidents. We explain what type of behaviour to expect and how to manage it. We look at how to anticipate problems – such as feeling terrified of the toilet – and the best way to deal with them before they arise. There are troubleshooting sections as well as information on common medical conditions that might need sorting out before your son can successfully come out of nappies.

Our method involves doing lots of preparation with your son from about 12 months. You gradually introduce the potty, then have potty-training 'sessions' during which your son goes without his nappy for an hour or two, slowly building up to being completely nappy-free (usually in a couple of weeks).

This makes our programme ideal for busy mums, including those who work or who have other children, because you can fit the 'sessions' around your hectic life. You don't even need to do a session every day – perhaps a few at the weekend and a couple during the week at bath time. Just do whatever suits you and your family setup.

GETTING THE TIMING RIGHT

Before you start potty training your son, we show you how to spot the signs that he's ready so you can get the timing exactly right. This is essential because if you start too young he'll find it too challenging, but leave it too late and he'll get bored.

You may have heard of mums who try potty training their babies from a few weeks old by holding them over the potty and making hissing noises until their infant wees. Such mothers argue that this is what many cultures around the world do because they don't have the money for disposable nappies and washing machines. They also point out how this method benefits the environment by not using hundreds of disposable nappies that end up in landfill sites.

Indeed, perhaps your own mother potty trained you when you were around 18 months, and she herself may have been potty trained even younger. Until recently it was fashionable to get babies out of nappies as young as possible. This makes lots of sense if you're using cloth nappies and don't have a washing machine or tumble drier, because every wee or poo in the potty means considerably less work. But training young toddlers and babies is a long, tedious process involving the mother 'catching' the wees rather than the child having much awareness of needing to go. So it's actually Mum who is trained to watch for signs that her tot is about to wee.

We think that with the benefit of disposable nappies, washing machines and laundry services, it's better to wait for your son to be truly ready to use the toilet – when he's physiologically developed enough. This will allow him to switch from nappies to the potty swiftly and be in control of going to the toilet by himself.

We hope that both you and your son will love our pressure-free training strategy. After all, potty training your toddler is the great milestone which takes a child from toddlerhood to the pre-school stage, and we want you both to find it a fun and positive experience.

If you don't rush it, potty training will actually take less time in the long run. Then you can start looking forward to the end of nappies. Just think – no more leaking messes to clean up or changing-table tantrums to deal with.

PENIS, WILLY OR PEE PEE?

You'll need to pick a 'name' from quite a young age. From about the age of one, little boys will notice that they have a penis and happily play with themselves on the changing table. This is the perfect opportunity to teach him what it's called.

By the way, don't try to stop your son touching his penis. He's far too young for this to be in any way sexual. He's simply exploring his body in the same way as he may play with his toes, belly button or his hair.

So what do you call his penis? It needs to be a name that will sound okay in front of other parents, your GP and other family members. And, more importantly, something that won't get him teased later on – so nothing too babyish.

We've used 'willy' for this book as it's what we've taught our sons to say. It's perhaps the most commonly used name for a penis. Everyone understands it, it's not babyish or embarrassing, and your son won't be teased.

Penis is probably the most politically correct name, and will get lots of approval from sexual health educators. And some people would argue that this is the only anatomically accurate name. Yet parents often refer to their children having full tummies rather than full stomachs so there's a reasonable argument for not feeling compelled to use the biologically correct term.

But even if you are in the minority of parents who are comfortable saying 'penis' to their young sons, and decide to teach him the 'proper' word, chances are you'll find this pretty much impossible. Because once he's chatting away to other kids at school, he'll probably start saying 'willy' or something similar and won't want mum and dad being 'weird' by saying penis.

There are lots of other names for a penis including 'winkle', 'pee pee' and 'wee wee'. Perhaps your family has a nickname that you're all used to and that's fine – just tell any carers and your son's nursery so that they understand him.

The same applies to what you call urine and faeces. We've chosen wee and poo. Although wee and poo aren't biological terms, everyone understands them, including doctors, teachers, grandparents and, most importantly, kids. Again, if you choose a family nickname, don't forget to explain to your son's carers to avoid any confusion.

1

Is Your Son Ready?

Timing is crucial to successful potty training. Get it right and potty training will be quick, tear-free and with few accidents. But time it wrong and you'll run into problems. Both you and your son will find the whole thing stressful and tedious and you'll feel like failures.

The average age in the UK for boys to start potty training is around two and a half, while for girls it's a few months earlier. An American study published in the journal *Pediatrics* found that training before the age of 27 months nearly always takes longer than training a child after this age.

Of course, children develop at their own pace. Your little boy could be ready to come out of nappies as young as 18 months, or may not be developed enough until he's three. So it's important to observe your son closely and only begin training when he's both physically and mentally ready.

Providing you time it right, we estimate that it should take only a couple of weeks of very relaxed potty training for your son to go dry most of the time, and for him to be able to tell you when he needs a wee or a poo. It will be a little longer before you can leave home without bothering to pack a spare pair of pants and trousers, 'just in case'. You can expect the occasional accident for a few months.

HOW TO TELL IF HE'S PHYSICALLY READY

To be toilet trained, your son must first be able to walk confidently, sit and stand up. Before this, he'll be too busy learning to use his voluntary muscles to be consistently aware of his bodily functions, and it would overload his system to attempt to potty-train him.

He also needs to control his bladder and bowel muscles, and if these aren't developed enough he simply won't succeed. Most children under the age of 20 months don't have sufficient bladder control to be potty trained, which means their bladders empty too often.

The bowel muscles tend to develop earlier than the bladder muscles, and you'll notice that between the age of one and two, your son does fewer poos and gradually starts pooing at around the same time each day.

Then, as the urethral sphincter muscles mature (which hold urine in the bladder), your son will go for longer without weeing and have a dry nappy for about three hours or longer. Most boys reach this stage of physical development by around two, although some will be later.

As well as a change in how frequently your son wees and poos, you can also expect to see him become aware of doing a wee or poo. So if he stops playing then squats or perhaps hides, it shows that he's aware of going to the toilet. This can happen between the ages of two and two and a half, and then you can expect your little boy to start announcing that he's having a wee or a poo.

CHECKLIST

Signs that Your Son is Physically Ready to Start Potty Training

☐ Older than 20 months

☐ Able to sit, stand and walk with ease

☐ Can walk up the stairs to the toilet (assuming it's upstairs in your home)

☐ Bowel movements are regular

☐ Stays dry for around three hours

HOW TO TELL IF HE'S MENTALLY READY

Being physically ready is only half the story – learning to use a potty also requires good language and communication skills. Because little boys tend to be mentally less mature than girls, it usually takes them longer to come out of nappies.

This is all to do with how male and female brains develop. Crudely speaking, boys tend to use the left-hand side of their brain which thinks analytically. Girls use both the left-hand side and also the creative right-hand side at the same time because the neural pathway between the left and right side is more efficient.

Using both sides of their brain is thought to give girls the edge when it comes to learning to talk. And girls' language skills are well known to be better than boys' until the age of five.

You'll find yourself chatting away as you encourage your son to sit on the potty. Then there will be lots more chat and praise if he succeeds. And your little boy will need to talk to you about needing the potty.

As well as having adequate language skills, your son should be mature enough to want to start using the potty or toilet – if he refuses to have a go at sitting on a potty he's telling you he's not mentally ready. Or he may be afraid of the toilet flushing or sitting on the toilet – this is more common amongst little boys than girls.

Signs that Your Son is Mentally Ready to Start Potty Training

☐ Able to talk and say 'I need a wee or a poo'

☐ Interested in other people going to the toilet, such as mum, dad and siblings

☐ Notices and tells you when he has soiled his nappy

☐ Stops what he's doing to poo in his nappy – perhaps squatting or hiding away

☐ Sometimes tells you when he's weeing in his nappy

☐ Enthusiastic about sitting on a potty, flushing the toilet, trying on big boy pants

ARE YOU READY?

Timing is everything when it comes to potty training. It's not only important for your son to be ready; you have to be ready as well. So don't even think about potty training if you're about to move house, have a baby, go on holiday, change your childcare arrangements or start a new job. Pick a time when you're just following your normal routine as this will mean that your stress levels will be low, and so will your son's.

Potty training requires time and patience so it's important to choose a time when things are calm – it's better to wait a couple of months and for it to be a happy, fun game, than to rush.

Don't Rush

It can be tempting to try and get your son out of nappies to fit in with other events, such as having another baby or before Christmas. Or perhaps your antenatal friends have successfully potty trained their children, or your mum's asking, 'Isn't it about time?'

A very common reason for pushing your son into potty training is that he's starting pre-school nursery at three and has to be out of nappies (*see page 31 on what to do if he really doesn't seem ready*).

By all means give potty training a go, especially if you think your son may be physically and mentally mature enough (*see the checklists above*). If it turns out that he's not ready, it will become apparent very quickly – you'll spend a couple of days trying to 'catch' wees and poos in the potty because your little boy seems totally clueless about what to do. He won't be able to anticipate when he needs to go, and will probably get irritated about having to sit on his potty. If this happens and it's obvious that potty training isn't working, then be prepared to wait another couple of months before trying again.

Unless your son has one or two successes – when he knows he's about to wee or poo, or seems very enthusiastic about sitting on the potty and waiting until he goes – don't be tempted to persevere. So many mums make this mistake because they're determined that their son should come out of nappies by a certain age or before a particular event. But little boys are very sensitive to feeling like a failure, and you'll end up setting up problems for the future.

Even if you do manage to potty train your son early in his second year, he's then more likely to have a setback and start refusing to use the potty later on than if you'd waited until he was nearer two and a half (*see Chapter 10*). Try to avoid potty training becoming a 'big deal'. It shouldn't stress you out, and certainly shouldn't upset your son.

DON'T WAIT TOO LONG

While it's important to wait until your son is mature enough before you start potty training him, be aware that there's a window of opportunity – usually sometime between the ages of two and three. It's easy to delay potty training because disposable nappies are so convenient, and there's less incentive to leave them behind than in the days of terry towelling nappies and no washing machines.

So you somehow keep finding excuses to postpone the big event – the most common one is waiting to potty train in the summer because accidents in the garden don't matter. But wait too long and you'll end up with a four-year-old who's still in nappies. Try not to fall into this trap of waiting because after the age of about three and a half you may find that your son is reluctant to give up the convenience of nappies, and his initial interest in pooing and weeing has long passed.

If your son struggles to leave nappies behind after the age of four, go and see your GP and ask for a referral to a specialist. It's important that your son is trained quickly because he'll be starting school. This will be problematic because teachers aren't prepared to change nappies, and if a child is wandering around with a soiled, smelly nappy the other children won't want to play with him.

Training in Time for Nursery

Many pre-school nurseries require children to be potty trained before they start at the age of three. This probably puts more pressure on parents to get their child potty trained than anything else, and it's particularly hard if you've got a son. It's essential that you don't put your little boy under pressure.

If he's just about potty trained but still has the occasional accident, explain this to his teacher – most nurseries have a ready supply of spare pants and trousers, and a few early accidents are part of everyday nursery life. It's likely that your son will become so involved with his new surroundings that he'll simply forget to go to the toilet – it's usual to see a bit of regression when children start nursery, particularly in boys. But if both you and his teachers remain relaxed, this is unlikely to be a problem for more than a term.

Some parents will struggle to get their son potty trained by three. If this is the case, consider postponing his nursery place by a term – a few months in the grand scheme of things isn't so important. Or you could talk to his teacher before he starts nursery who should be able to give you some reassurance and possibly provide practical help during the nursery day. Perhaps your son could wear nappies for the first few weeks while he settles in and go into pants after that.

Then you could go with him to the toilet when you arrive – this will help him to stay dry if he does a wee and will also give him the confidence to use the nursery toilets. Most little boys enjoy this extra bit of mummy or daddy attention and will happily cooperate, especially if you admire the nursery's mini-sized toilets and say how grown-up it all is. Many parents find that once they've spoken to the nursery teacher and know they have a little more time to 'train' their son, they relax and he's suddenly out of nappies.

2

Early Preparation for Potty Training (from 12 months)

I f you've gone through the checklists in Chapter 1 and realised that your son isn't ready to begin potty training, then we suggest you follow our early preparation programme which can start from as young as 12 months. Follow our guidelines and you'll find that when you come to actually potty train your son at about the age of two and a half, it will be a lot quicker and easier.

This two-stage programme aims firstly to give your son plenty of positive exposure to poos, wees and toilets so that by the time he starts potty training he understands basic bodily functions and is familiar with toilets. Secondly, it gives your son a bit of practice sitting on a potty and controlling his wee when he's in the bath.

With a few simple steps you can start showing your son some of the basics – such as how to sit on a potty, what a toilet is for, and even how he can hold his willy when he wees.

STAGE ONE – POSITIVE EXPOSURE TO POOS, WEES AND TOILETS

Your attitude to poo, wee and going to the toilet is crucial to your son's future success in potty training. It's important to teach him about the whole process of going to the toilet without giving any negative messages.

Let Your Son See His Dirty Nappy

Sometimes when you are changing your son show him the soiled nappy and explain how you're putting it in a nappy bag and cleaning the poo off his bottom. Or if you use cloth nappies, he can watch you put the poo down the toilet and wash the nappies.

You can also let him feel the heavy weight of a wet nappy, explaining how he's done lots of wee, and comparing it to a dry nappy.

This not only teaches your son that he does wees and poos, it also demonstrates that it's a natural process and nothing to be ashamed of. It's important never to show any disgust, however smelly or leaky his nappy happens to be.

Conceal Any Feelings of Disgust if Your Son Ever 'Plays' with His Poo

It's quite common for young children to wake up in their cots, take their nappies off then play with or even eat the poo. There's no getting away from the fact that this is disgusting, but don't freak out. Your son doesn't have a behavioural problem and he's not 'naughty'; he's simply being inquisitive. If it happens repeatedly, put him in a back-to-front sleep suit – he'll struggle to get the poppers undone and hopefully won't be able to get to his nappy. When cleaning up any mess – which can look like some sort of 'dirty protest' with poo on the bedclothes and even the walls – it's crucial that you remain calm and positive throughout. Showing shock, revulsion or anger – or panicking unnecessarily – will all send confusing or negative messages to your son.

Worse still, a condition called 'withholding constipation' can be a problem for toddlers (*see Chapter 9*). One reason is that parents and carers have expressed revulsion about the child's poo, usually because they find nappies and 'accidents' disgusting.

It's worth bearing in mind that mums find the smell of their own baby's poo less offensive than that of other people's babies, according to a study published in the *Journal of Evolution and Human Behaviour*

(July 2006). Mothers were given 'anonymous' nappies and they consistently reported that the ones belonging to their own baby were 'less revolting' than those of other people's children. The researchers suggested that the disgust instinct is perhaps overridden in mothers, as it would be dangerous for their babies if their mothers found them repellent.

Remember that other people may genuinely find changing your son's nappy more difficult than you do. Keep an eye on carers who change your son's nappy – make sure that they are relaxed and don't have hang-ups that your son could pick up on.

Take Him to the Loo with You

Most mums and dads take their babies to the loo with them because it's easier than leaving them crying outside. Don't break this habit as your son gets older – let him watch you on the toilet. There's no need to feel embarrassed. From about the age of one he'll simply be curious in the same innocent way he's curious if you crack an egg into a bowl, or fill the car up with petrol.

Don't worry about confusing him because you sit to wee whereas he'll eventually stand up. He'll have to sit on the toilet to poo when the time comes, and most boys learn to sit and wee first.

There will be times when you leave your little boy outside the loo, hammering on the door and howling. Don't worry about it – he'll survive for a few minutes and recover within moments of seeing you again. Indeed, we suggest you don't take your tot to the toilet with you every time you go or he'll come to expect it.

As long as he watches you on the loo quite often, your son will not only get an idea about what to do, he'll also learn not to be frightened of toilets. Boys can be particularly apprehensive when it comes to sitting on the loo at potty-training age, and some are even scared of flushing, thinking that they're going to be sucked away.

So make the most of his curiosity while he's still very young, letting him play with toilet paper (within reason!) and helping you flush the loo. He'll think the whole process is one big game and won't end up with toilet hang-ups. Your son will also enjoy washing his hands afterwards, so get him into good habits now.

It's particularly important to show little boys how to flush because if they can do this themselves it will give them a sense of control and help prevent them becoming frightened of being 'sucked away' later on. Also, if flushing is established as a bit of a treat it will help avoid the problem of your son getting upset when his poo is flushed away once he starts toilet training.

Plenty of little boys are so proud of what they produce in the potty that they'd rather play with it than flush it down the loo.

Encourage Him to Go to the Toilet with Dad

Watching Dad go for a wee is particularly helpful for little boys. He'll be able to see how the mechanics of the male body operate – how Dad stands up, holds his willy, aims his wee down the toilet, and gives his willy a shake afterwards. Men do all this without even thinking about it. And letting little boys watch their Dad is the most natural way for them to learn.

But lots of men simply refuse to take their sons to the loo with them. And even if they do, they may find the fascinated, wide-eyed stare a little disconcerting. Just remember, little boys will be a lot more curious the first few times they get to watch; after this their interest won't be quite so intense.

Another problem is that little boys are quite likely to want to 'touch Daddy's willy' – or try to touch the stream of wee – which obviously freaks most Dads out. But if Dad calmly says, 'No, you can't touch Daddy's willy but you can flush the toilet afterwards,' your son should hopefully be appeased.

If Dad refuses point blank to have an audience,

there are plenty of other ways to teach your son. The obvious alternative is for him to watch older brothers, cousins or friends – the earliest that children become modest is at around four years, and lots of little boys will happily wee in front of an audience much later than this.

If there isn't a male role model for him to watch, it's still pretty straightforward for Mum to teach her little boy everything he needs to know (*see Chapter 4*).

STAGE TWO – FUN WAYS FOR EARLY PRACTICE

Have a Potty in the Bathroom

From as young as 18 months you can have a potty in the bathroom for your son to play with when he's naked before his bath. He won't wee in it, but it's no bad thing for him to see the potty and gradually have a go at sitting on it.

You can buy a potty from your local pharmacy for a few pounds and keep it in a corner in the bathroom. There's no point buying anything fancy or making a big deal about this. Your son is probably a year off actually being able to use a potty, and it's essential that you stay relaxed and keep everything low-key.

When he's wandering around naked before his bath, simply show him the potty, tell him what it's for and what it's called, and say that he can sit on it if he wants to. If he does happen to sit on it then give him lots of praise, but if he's not interested, leave the potty in the corner and try to forget about it for a few months. He's got well over a year to become curious.

You can also keep a potty next to the toilet so that he can have a go at sitting on it and 'copying' when you go – you don't have to undress him for this; he can sit on the potty fully clothed.

There is absolutely no rush at this stage – it's more about having a potty in your home, just as you would if he had an older sibling. If your son has brothers and sisters who are just a couple of years older than him it's a big advantage when it comes to potty training. For a start he'll know what a potty is for, and he'll also be desperate to be 'big' like them, which will spur him on to learn.

Weeing in the Bath

This is a fun game that boys can play from about 18 months. It gives excellent practice at controlling their wee and teaches them to become aware of when they are about to wee.

All little children wee in the bath. You shouldn't try to stop it because you'll be giving negative messages. You can begin from around 18 months when he'll probably be able to stand up in the bath easily – use a bath mat to stop him slipping over. If you make sure that he's had plenty to drink at teatime, then he'll probably start weeing as soon as his feet go in the bath water – a common reflex response amongst small children.

Your son will be quite fascinated by weeing – encourage this because awareness is an early stage of control. So plenty of, 'Oh look, you're doing a wee, clever boy...' It's so easy to encourage him in the bath because you can see what's going on – in nappies you have no idea. And don't worry about the hygiene aspect – urine is sterile and won't do any harm at all.

Then you can use a small plastic cup or beaker, and as you 'catch' your son's wee he'll gradually realise that he is somehow involved in the weeing process. Try suggesting that he holds his willy to aim at the cup more accurately. Over the months, you'll see your son learn to anticipate when he's about to wee.

From around the age of two, your son may some-times be able to predict when he's about to wee. He'll slowly become more practised at this and eventually will be able to predict his wees; he may even ask for a cup and hold his willy to aim accurately in anticipation. If this happens it's a definite sign that he's ready to start potty training. However, this is a very slow process and takes months. It's likely that your son will ask for the cup quite often but nothing happens. In this case simply say, 'Perhaps the wee will come another day,' and change the subject. It's essential to keep this a game, and there should be no pressure. And remember that if your son's progress is particularly slow and he shows little interest in weeing in a cup, just forget about it. Like having a potty in the bathroom, this isn't a key part of potty training, just something that can be helpful for some little boys.

Encouraging Your Son to Wee in the Bath

When paediatricians need a urine sample they'll often give the child a drink 20 minutes beforehand, make sure the child is standing as this encourages weeing, run water (you can run the sink tap), and perhaps put the child's hand in water to bombard his senses with wetness. Doctors also use these techniques for adults suffering from urinary retention. If you try all these measures and your son doesn't wee, then don't worry because it doesn't work with everyone. But there's still a good chance there will be a wee in the bath every couple of weeks or so.

Public Toilets

It's all very well letting your little boy crawl around the toilet floor at home while you use the toilet, but this isn't advisable if you need to visit a public toilet, which can obviously be very dirty. The easiest thing to do in this case is to find a disabled toilet and wheel him into the cubicle in his buggy. He can still watch, but can't touch anything.

If this isn't possible then you'll have to learn the trick of holding your son in one arm and going to the loo one-handed. This is just about possible although you can forget doing up your trouser zip.

Then when your son gets too big to hold and also learns to walk, from around 13 months, you've got the problem of him wanting to play with the sanitary bin, undoing the lock on the door, and touching the seat as he squeezes round the back of the loo. All highly stressful and pretty unhygienic, but try not to show too much revulsion as you want to avoid your son associating toilets with being told off and yelled at. Try to remain firm but calm and wash his hands very well afterwards.

Once your son is old enough to use the loo himself, wipe the seat beforehand – whether he's sitting or standing – as he's bound to touch it. One tip is to let him stand on your feet so he's tall enough to wee into the toilet.

Dads can take their sons into the gents to try out a urinal – the type with an open metal tray that goes down to the ground are fairly easy for small boys to use – and it's hard for them to miss when aiming. Some public toilets have smaller, lowered ceramic urinals for boys, although even then a child will often need to be at least three or four to use them properly. An alternative when using an adult urinal is that Dad simply holds his son up to the required height, and also helps out with any aiming issues.

3

Countdown to the Big Day

When you are confident that your son is physically and mentally mature enough to begin potty training, you can tell him what's about to happen. Pick your moment carefully – ideally when he's calm and receptive – and emphasise what a big boy he will be when he uses the potty and toilet.

Explain that soon he's going to wear big boy pants instead of nappies, and that he's going to do his wees and poos in the potty or toilet. Suggest that you go to the shops together to buy the pants and two more potties, and make this into a special event. You've probably already got a potty in the bathroom (as we suggested in our pre-training tips in Chapter 2). But this won't go to waste as it's useful to have spare potties around when you're training. Do go potty shopping with your little boy to mark the event and make him feel important.

If you've judged it right and your little boy really is ready to begin, he'll find everything to do with potties, toilets and big boy pants very interesting. Chat about potty training every now and then over the next few days, but keep it brief and light. Little boys quickly pick up on any desperation to get them to succeed, which they can find quite stressful. Your aim is to get him interested but not alarmed.

SHOPPING LIST

There is an overwhelming array of potty-training gadgets on the market, and only a few are of much use. Here's our pick of what you need, and also what you don't. Remember to let your son help choose some of these items – particularly the pants and potties – because if he feels involved he's more likely to cooperate once potty training begins.

A Couple of Cheap Plastic Potties (identical if possible)

You'll need one in the bathroom and another in the play area. The reason we suggest getting identical ones is so that you don't get into a situation where your son only wants to use the 'yellow' potty. Let him choose the colour. We suggest cheap potties (a few pounds) because, being small, they are easy to empty and clean, and they encourage your son to squat with his feet on the floor which makes it easier to poo than sitting on one of the larger-style potties.

Most potties have splashguards or a lip – make sure that your son sits with this at the front. Avoid detachable splashguards as boys have been known to scratch themselves on them, and they are also more difficult to clean.

A Child's Toilet Seat

Imagine sitting on a toilet that's about twice as big as you're used to. You'd have to be a bit of an acrobat to stay on, let alone go to the loo at the same time. A special child toilet seat scales down the toilet to toddler size, helping your little boy to balance and also feel safe.

A Stepping Stool

Your son can stand on this to reach the toilet, and also the sink for washing his hands. You can buy cheap plastic stools made especially for children.

Big Boy Pants

Your little boy should definitely be involved in choosing these. If he insists on a favourite character, like Bob the Builder or Lunar Jim, that's great as he'll be really keen to wear them. Get pants in a bigger size than he needs so that they're easier to pull up and down.

Trousers

You can buy trousers with elasticated waists so that your son will eventually find going to the toilet by himself easier than if he has to cope with buttons and zips (jogging bottoms work well). And forget about dungarees – too complicated for children.

Stickers

Star charts and reward stickers are extremely useful and provide an incentive by giving your son something to aim for, as well as a feeling of fulfilment after a successful potty or toilet session.

A Bathroom Mat

Get one with a soft top side and a rubber or plastic bottom. This is a clever way to protect sofas – just put the bathroom mat on the sofa for your son to sit on. It is particularly useful if your son tends to wet himself while watching television. The mat is soft for your son to sit on, yet plastic backed and machine washable.

WHAT NOT TO WASTE YOUR MONEY ON

Expensive Toilet-lookalike Potties

These are as big as chairs and have lids, and are probably more comfortable than standard potties and perhaps more appealing to young children. But in our opinion they are a waste of money because if your son is ready to begin toilet training, he'll only be using the potty briefly in the early stages before happily using the toilet. Our training programme encourages moving from the potty to the toilet as quickly as possible.

Themed Potties

For the same reason we advise against buying animal-themed and musical potties. If your son needs this sort of persuasion to sit on a potty, he's not yet ready to begin training.

Pull-up Nappies

Most children simply continue to wee and poo in these – and changing a soiled pull-up is far messier than an ordinary nappy because as you pull it down the poo gets smeared down your child's legs.

Having said that, pull-ups can sometimes be useful for night training *(see Chapter 8)*, and also for those occasions when your son is determined to be grown-up but you want him to wear a nappy, such as for a long car journey *(see Chapter 6)*.

Training Pants

These are absorbent, but look more grown-up and like real pants than a nappy. They are designed not to leak but to make your son feel wet so that he becomes more aware of when he's pooing or weeing. Boys, however, are less likely to mind feeling wet than girls, and tend to carry on weeing away as though they are still in nappies. If you begin potty training when your son is ready, he'll already be pretty aware of when he's pooing or weeing. Training pants tend to be used as a prop when parents try to potty train their children too young.

Portable Potties

These are fold-flat potties with plastic bags and nappy-like pads to absorb wee and poo. So when you're out and about you can unfold the potty, then once your son has done a wee or poo you wrap up the contents in the bag and throw it away.

We say don't bother with these, though, because one advantage with little boys is that if they need a wee, they can go pretty much anywhere – trees, drains, lampposts and so on. For the very few emergency poos when you're out and can't find a toilet, just carry a spare nappy.

Portable Loo Seats

These are designed to be placed over public loos that may be very dirty. But we say you don't need these for little boys because they don't have to sit on public toilets to wee, and it's not worth the trouble for the few public-loo poos that they will have. You're better off carrying wipes for the seat, and antibacterial hand gel to wash hands well afterwards.

PLAYING WITH THE 'NEW TOYS'

If you've followed our early preparation tips in Chapter 2, then your son has probably already had a go at playing with a potty. But do let him admire his new potties, and he can help put them in place in the bathroom and play area.

He can now have a play with the other things you've bought before you actually begin potty training. Show him the pants – he can try them on if he wants to and admire himself in front of a mirror, or you can put them on teddies. You can also start using the booster step for hand washing, and if he wants to he can try sitting on his child's toilet seat.

As with all new toys, you'll find that he's interested in some but not others, and that they lose their appeal pretty quickly. That's fine; simply have them in place for D-day when you start potty training – so pants in his drawer, toilet seat on the toilet, potties in place in the bathroom and play area.

Try to start actual potty training within about a week so that there is still some novelty value.

THE DAY BEFORE YOU BEGIN

Before you start day one of our potty-training programme, there are a number of decisions and issues you need to be clear about to ensure things go smoothly. Here we guide you through all the questions that may arise.

Teach Your Son to Wee Sitting Down

We think it's better to teach your son to wee sitting down rather than standing up because it requires less skill and keeps things a bit more straightforward in the beginning. Also, little boys often don't know if they are about to wee or poo so it's easier to get them sitting on the potty as soon as they realise that 'something' is about to happen. Most importantly, when they are having a poo it's very likely that they will have a wee at the same time (and will continue to do this all their lives). So little boys do need to learn how to wee sitting down – holding their willies to avoid mess – as well as standing up.

Some would argue that if you teach your son to wee sitting down, you'll later have to show him how to wee standing up, and that this is something else for him to learn. However, in our programme you move from sitting to standing quite quickly.

Don't Skip the Potty Stage

Some parents choose to teach their son to use the toilet from day one of him coming out of nappies instead of starting with a potty. The benefits are not having to clean a dirty potty, and not having to make the transfer from the potty to the toilet.

However, we recommend starting with a potty then moving reasonably swiftly to the toilet (*see Chapter 5*). Potties have the advantage of putting a child in a squatting position with his feet on the floor, and this helps the body to poo.

Also, a child is likely to sit for a little longer on a potty than a toilet, and this increases the chances of him actually weeing or pooing successfully, rather than having an accident a couple of minutes later. Finally, you won't have to hover over your son, as potties are easier to sit on than toilets, and this will help him to feel more independent.

Take Your Time

Some mums opt to just 'go for it'. They pick a day their son comes out of nappies and that's it – no more nappies at home, out in the buggy or in the car. The theory behind this approach is that although it's messy for a week or two, children stay focused and learn quickly. That way, you get potty training over and done with.

But the 'go for it' technique requires rearranging your diary to be at home with your son for a couple of weeks, perhaps taking time off work, and avoiding visits to family or friends who have carpets and sofas.

Although this method may work for some, chances are that you'll find it quite stressful, and little boys are highly sensitive to any tension and are likely to play up. Also, as they tend to learn more slowly than girls, we recommend a slower, more relaxed approach for boys.

Choose and Prepare a Location

If the room your son usually plays in has a wooden or easily washable floor, or perhaps old carpets, then this is ideal. Remember that you can put a bathroom mat on the sofa (the soft side is nice for him to sit on while the rubber backing will protect your sofa).

If you've had your home re-carpeted recently, you could set up a play area in the corner of the kitchen if you've got the space. Or buy several plastic-backed bathmats to protect your new floor along with some cheap rugs. Make sure the room you choose is warm enough for semi-naked toddlers – perhaps turn up the heating by a degree or two if it's chilly outside.

The garden, if you've got one, is a good place to begin potty training as you can encourage your son to 'water the flowers' and there's no clearing up unless he does a poo. So it's no surprise that many mums wait until summer. Do take a potty into the garden in case he wants to do a poo, and you may find that he's happier weeing in his potty than on the plants – all little boys are different.

4

D-day

I f you are confident that your son is ready to come out of nappies, you've been shopping for his big boy pants and he knows exactly what a potty is, then here's how to begin.

Our method involves potty training your son in 'sessions'. These last for about an hour or perhaps longer, depending on how your son responds. During a session your son goes without his nappy, at home initially, then at the end of the session you put his nappy back on again.

Because he's only without a nappy for a short space of time, it takes the stress away. This is crucial because if your son picks up on your anxiety it will affect his confidence and could make the whole potty-training process miserable for him. And this will affect how quickly he learns.

Some people say that it is confusing to switch back and forth from nappies to pants, but we've not found this to be the case. Even with the more intense potty-training methods, mums pop a nappy back on their tots at naptime and bedtime, and children seem to cope well with the switch.

If you follow our 'potty-training sessions' approach, there will be very few accidents and hopefully no tears. It may take a little longer than other methods – probably two to six weeks depending on how many sessions you fit in and how quickly your son learns – but because it's such a relaxed way to learn, the chances of future problems and setbacks are minimised.

A STEP-BY-STEP GUIDE TO A TYPICAL POTTY-TRAINING SESSION

1. How to Begin

In the morning when you dress your son, simply ask him if he'd like to wear big boy pants today. If a morning session doesn't fit in with your schedule, then you could have your first potty-training session in the afternoon after your son's nap when he'll be feeling refreshed. As you change his nappy after his nap, again suggest that he may like to put big boy pants on.

Don't try to 'time' your sessions to fit in with when he usually has a poo as this will create expectation and anxiety. It's more important for the sessions to take place when your son is feeling happy, usually when he's not hungry or overtired, so that he'll associate potty-training sessions with having fun.

If he says 'Yes' to big boy pants

Move on to step 2 below.

If he says 'No'

Try to stay relaxed. As an alternative, ask if he'd like to wear no pants and no nappy and have a go at using his potty today. If he says 'Yes', move on to step 2 below, but if he still refuses then say, 'Maybe another day.' You'll probably feel frustrated as you're all psyched up to begin, but waiting a few more days or even weeks makes no difference to the end result.

Alternatively, you could have a go at bath time when your little boy won't be wearing a nappy anyway. Try going up to the bathroom half an hour early and bring some toys to keep your son amused before his bath. Then follow our programme from step 3 below.

2. What Should He Wear?

Assuming that your son has agreed to putting on his big boy pants, then help him into them and explain that he's a big boy and because he's not wearing a nappy he can wee or poo in the potty.

You can also put him in a T-shirt plus a pair of socks to help keep him warm. Being semi-naked will actually help your son to remember to use the potty – you'll also notice immediately if he starts weeing or pooing and can pop him on the potty before he's finished. Bundling him up in trousers during the early stages will feel more secure and nappy-like, making him more likely to forget that he needs to use his potty.

Once your son is in his pants and ready to begin, you can remind him where his potty is in his play area.

3. Give Him a Drink

Offering your son a drink at the beginning of the session can get things going. It takes about 20 minutes from giving a child a drink to them needing a wee. And you'll know roughly what time of day his poos tend to happen, although this isn't an exact science, so just accept that when it happens it happens.

4. Sitting on the Potty

Suggest that your little boy tries sitting on the potty (if you've followed our pre-training guide he'll be used to doing this). If he's wearing pants explain that you have to pull these down so that they don't get wet – if he's got a favourite character on his pants tell him you don't want to get 'Bob the Builder' or similar wet. Give him masses of praise just for sitting. Then ask if he needs to do a wee or a poo. He'll probably say no in which case you just say, 'Maybe later.'

5. Watching out for Wees

Play together and keep an eye on him. Little boys often hold their willies if they need a wee, so this is a good time to remind him.

Suggest every 30 minutes or so that he sits on the potty. If he refuses, simply say, 'Maybe later.' Don't remind him more often than this as it will probably annoy him and feel as though you're pressurising him. And don't try and make him sit there for more than about 30 seconds as it will be uncomfortable and boring for him. Although some experts suggest playing games or watching DVDs to keep tots on the potty long enough to wee, our training programme isn't about catching a wee by chance. It's all about your son being ready to have some bladder and bowel control and knowing when he needs to go.

6. His First Accident

It's quite likely that his first wee or poo will be on the floor or in his pants. But stay very positive – 'Oh look, you've done a wee, and because you're not wearing a nappy there's a puddle on the floor. Next time you can do a wee in the…' Let your son fill in the word 'potty' and keep the whole thing a fun game. React in a similarly positive way if he poos on the floor. Above all, stay positive and give praise.

Clean up quickly, so have dry pants and wipes to hand. If he's done a poo, put his soiled pants in a nappy bag then later you can scrape the poo into the toilet before rinsing the pants in a bucket and machine-washing them. Wipe his bottom with wipes just as though you're cleaning him up after a dirty nappy.

7. His First Wee or Poo in the Potty

If he wees or poos in the potty, then make a tremendous fuss and dish out praise. Clap, give him a kiss, call anyone else in the house to come and have a look at his wee/poo, phone Grandma to tell her. This is quite a good time to end the first training session – stop on a high and ask if he'd like to have another go later/tomorrow. He's bound to say yes after all that praise. By all means continue if you and your son want to. Perhaps you can keep the nappy off until it's time for lunch, going out or a nap.

You'll soon discover that when your son sits to wee, it can be very messy. Splashguards on potties help to a certain extent, but your son will need to hold his willy and aim downwards. You'll probably have to do this for him at first because he'll have enough to concentrate on. Don't be surprised if it seems odd holding your son's willy while he wees. Most mums admit it's a bit strange initially but after about 10 trips to the potty or toilet you won't even think about it.

As long as you've timed it right and your son is well and truly ready to begin potty training, you'll find that he's very receptive and will quickly learn to hold his own willy if you show him how. He'll learn particularly quickly if he's been playing the 'weeing in the bath' game (*see Chapter 2*).

8. Clean the Potty

Tip the wee or poo down the loo and wipe it out with toilet paper. Then use antibacterial wipes. You can give it a thorough rinse with an antibacterial agent at the end of the day, but when you rinse, do tip the water down the toilet rather than the sink!

How Many Sessions?

You can have as many or as few potty-training sessions in a day as you choose – just be led by your son and what he wants to do. Fit the sessions in with your schedule and what works with the rest of the family because if you are relaxed, your son will be too. If you miss a day or two it doesn't matter – just pick up where you left off.

TROUBLESHOOTING

He Doesn't Wee or Poo at All During His Session

This is quite common, and you may well find that as soon as you pop a nappy back on your son at the end of the session, he instantly does a wee or a poo. If he didn't have any accidents during the session then it could be that he was feeling a bit anxious without his nappy and was hanging on until he was wearing it again. This is actually a good sign as it shows that your little boy has some control.

Over the next few sessions your son should gain more confidence and will probably start using the potty very soon. In the meantime, try to remain calm and keep encouraging him. Let him set the pace, and before the sessions do ask him if he'd like to wear his big boy pants and try his potty. If he says no, simply say, 'Maybe later,' and be prepared to leave potty training for a few days. Letting him feel in control is the best way to build his confidence.

He Has Accidents

It's perfectly natural for him to have an accident or two during his first session. The trick is gauging whether it's because he's clueless as to when he's about to wee or poo because he's still too immature, or that he simply became too involved in what he was doing to concentrate on his bladder and bowel.

If he's ever managed to predict when he's about to wee, such as when in the bath, then he's probably mature enough, so continue with the sessions and reminding him to sit on the potty. But if he's never announced that he's about to wee or poo and seems slightly irritated and frustrated by potty training, there's a good chance he's not yet ready. Try another couple of short sessions and, if there's no change, postpone potty training for a few weeks. The joy of this method is that a session only takes around an hour so it's easy enough to give it a quick go every now and then to see if your son is ready.

He Won't Sit on His Potty

This may be your son's way of telling you that he's not mentally mature enough to start potty training yet, in which case stop the sessions and try again in a few weeks.

There's always the possibility that he doesn't like the colour or style of his potty if it's different to the one he's used to playing with in the bathroom. So do ask him if he'd like to sit on the other potty – you may be pleasantly surprised.

He Refuses to Wear Pants

Again, this can be a sign that your son isn't yet ready to start potty training. Don't force him into pants; just try him with nothing on his bottom half. Sometimes it takes little boys a few weeks to want to wear pants because it's all too much to cope with at first.

Occasionally, this problem can be resolved by choosing a different 'character' on his pants. It's worth another trip to the shops to see if anything different appeals to him. Don't worry if you end up with lots of pants that he refuses to wear, as once your son is really ready to start potty training they'll all get plenty of use.

5

The Next Few Weeks

f your first potty-training session went well and your son seemed cheerful about it, then here's how to continue.

Do note that although we've called the following sections days two to four, weeks two, three and so on, these are optimistic estimates. All little boys are different and learn at different rates. So be led by your son rather than an urge to 'keep up', and move to each new stage only when your son seems ready.

DAYS TWO TO FOUR – WEEING AND POOING IN HIS POTTY

After a few days of having 'potty sessions' with your son, you'll have a pretty good idea about whether it's working. The important thing is that you're both enjoying the sessions and not finding them stressful. If your son seems annoyed, irritated or uncooperative during the sessions, it almost certainly means that he's not yet ready, so pack away the pants before potty training turns into a battle, and try again in a few weeks.

What You Can Expect

During the early sessions your son may sit on his potty and do either a wee or a poo with or without being reminded.

How You Can Help Your Son

Continue to fit potty sessions around your schedule, perhaps introducing a couple a day if things seem to be going well. There's no need to progress the sessions in the first few days; just let your son enjoy being a 'clever boy' and give him lots of praise.

Rewarding is key to encouraging your little boy to leave his nappies behind, so keep the praise coming. Try using a star chart – most mums use them for something at some stage because kids love them and they work, so it's definitely worth a go. Make it very easy for your son to get stars – just sitting on the potty, putting on his big boy pants and washing his hands all get stars. This will help him to feel like a success from the start. When he makes real progress –

like actually doing a wee or poo in his potty, or telling you that he needs the potty – make more fuss of him than ever. Perhaps put bigger stars on his chart or favourite stickers.

DAYS FIVE TO SEVEN – ASKING FOR THE POTTY

Some time during the first week, there's a chance that your son will actually anticipate when he's about to do a wee or poo and ask for the potty. This shows that he's aware of signals from his bladder or bowels, able to communicate that he needs the potty, and can physically hang on long enough to make it to the potty.

What You Can Expect

Asking for the potty is quite likely to happen during the first week, and if not then in week two. If your son is younger than about two and a half then it will probably take him longer, so give him all the time he needs. And do make allowances if your little boy happens to be slower than average to grasp potty training – just ask yourself, does it really matter if it takes him a few months longer?

How You Can Help Your Son

Your aim is to keep the sessions fun and make potty training a positive experience, rather than racing to the finish and possibly giving him hang-ups in the process. So ensure that you follow your son's lead by moving on to the next step when he is ready rather than when you are.

Confidence Trick

When you empty your son's potty down the toilet, let him flush it as part of his clever boy reward – 'You're such a clever boy to have done a wee/poo in your potty, would you like to flush the toilet?' Close the seat so that he can climb up and he'll associate getting on the loo as a reward rather than something frightening.

THE SECOND WEEK – FROM POTTY TO TOILET

Once your son is able to ask for the potty, he's ready to progress and you can start teaching him to move from the potty to the toilet.

As discussed in Chapter 3, we recommend teaching

your son to sit to wee before he learns to stand up and wee – mainly because there's a reasonable chance that he'll need to poo and wee at the same time. Also, the sooner he learns to be confident about sitting on a toilet the better, as you'll discover when you're out and about and he needs a poo.

What You Can Expect

If you keep the pressure to an absolute minimum, you'll probably find that your son is happy to give sitting on the toilet a go within a couple of days. But even if he takes a few weeks, it really doesn't matter. Just remember that using an upstairs toilet, rather than using the potty in his play area, will obviously require a bit more control, and an extra week or two can make all the difference.

How You Can Help Your Son

The easiest way to get him started on the toilet is during bath-time potty sessions. He'll already be used to his bath-time potty and will be undressed for his bath, so sitting on the toilet won't be that big a deal. And there will be no rushing upstairs for a wee as you'll both already be in the bathroom.

If you've followed our pre-training tips, then your son will already know what a toilet is for, and rather than 'teaching' him, all you have to do is ask him if he'd like to try sitting on the toilet instead of the potty next time he needs to go. He's very likely to say no as this can seem like quite a big step, but once again you can say, 'Okay, maybe next time,' which lets him determine his own rate of progress.

Continue to give him lots of praise when he sits on his potty – he mustn't feel that he's done anything 'wrong' by not having the courage to sit on the loo. But after his wee you could try suggesting that he practises just sitting on the toilet so that he 'might be able to do a wee in the toilet another day'. If he shows any reluctance, quickly move on to something else that is not potty related – such as a toy or activity in

Keep the Potty

Don't even think about banning his potty as it's become his symbol of success, and he'd feel very insecure if it suddenly disappeared. In fact, it's no bad thing to have a potty sitting around long after your son has learnt to use the toilet. If he chooses to use it sometimes, that's fine – none of us achieves our maximum capability all the time. Continue to praise him – there's nothing wrong with using his potty.

a different room – and don't mention sitting on the toilet for the rest of the day. You don't want this to become a stressful sticking point.

But if he's willing to sit for a few moments, give him the usual overdose of praise and a gold star. Then the next time he asks for his potty, you can again suggest that he tries sitting on the loo.

THE THIRD WEEK – WEEING STANDING UP

We suggest that you teach your son how to stand and wee once he is happy about sitting on the toilet.

What You Can Expect

If your son can watch Dad or another male role model, he'll probably want to copy within a few days. Teaching him yourself may take longer but is straightforward enough. Even if your son is slow to learn to wee standing up, we can pretty much guarantee that when he starts nursery or school he'll soon pick it up because he'll be desperate to be like the other boys.

How You Can Help Your Son

Don't even think about getting your son to stand up and wee in the potty because it will obviously be very messy. Instead, ask him if he'd like to try weeing in the toilet while standing up (like Daddy). If Daddy isn't involved then simply explain to your son that men and boys wee standing up, holding their willies.

Don't be disappointed if at first your son wants to remain seated – it's important that he progresses at his own pace. But you'll probably find that after a week or so he'll have a go at standing up, and if Dad is involved your son will probably want to try after a few days.

When your son agrees, show him how to climb up on to the stool, hold his willy and aim for the water to avoid spills. To make this fun, try putting 'targets' down the loo. Cornflakes and torn-up toilet paper work well and your little boy will love trying to wee on them. Show your son how to shake the wee off his willy afterwards.

Once your little boy is confident about climbing up on his stool and weeing down the toilet, you can teach him about lifting up the seat, wiping any spills and putting the seat down afterwards. Be particularly careful with the seat because a sudden slam can frighten him, or worse, hurt him badly if his willy gets trapped.

If this happens, be prepared for a setback as your son will feel genuinely anxious about using the toilet. Let him return to the toilet in his own time, and if he was particularly badly hurt or frightened you could even consider buying a slow-closing toilet seat that glides down shut and can't fall and slam quickly. You can pick these up at large DIY stores or specialist bathroom shops.

Awkward Questions

As you teach your son about sitting and standing to wee, don't be surprised if he asks a few 'technical' questions. You'll no doubt find yourself explaining that mummy doesn't have a willy; that, unlike mummy, boys don't need to wipe after a wee – they just shake; and how men and boys stand to wee but ladies and girls sit down. Try not to be embarrassed and answer his questions as accurately and straightforwardly as possible – after all, your son is simply curious. Ignoring the questions or replying with vague answers will only confuse him.

Extra Aiming Practice

Weeing in the bath is a great opportunity for your son to practise his aim (*see Chapter 2*). You can also encourage outdoors weeing. If it's warm enough, then your son can play in the garden (or a park) in his pants and you can play a game of watering the plants, trees or the grass. Suggest that he holds his willy (help him if necessary) and aims downwards at something about a foot in front of him to avoid too much wee going down his legs.

6

The Fourth Week and Beyond – Out and About

THE FOURTH WEEK – YOUR FIRST TRIP OUT

Before venturing out, we recommend that your son is able to do the following:

1. He can anticipate that he needs a wee or poo and tell you so.
2. He is confident about sitting on a toilet.
3. He can wee standing up.
4. He rarely wears a nappy at home.
5. He doesn't have more accidents if he's wearing trousers rather than just pants.

(Please note that if your little boy has learnt to use the potty and toilet while wandering around in just his pants, once you put trousers on him he's likely to start having accidents because he'll feel bundled up and secure and may forget that he needs to ask for the potty. So allow a few extra sessions at home while he gets used to wearing trousers and give him a few reminders.)

Until you can tick all of the above, we don't think there's much point in going out without a nappy because the chances of your little boy having an accident will still be pretty high – and cleaning up in public is stressful. Having said that, plenty of mums following the 'all or nothing' approach grit their teeth and carry a potty in the buggy for a few weeks to catch any emergencies. But we think that waiting a few more weeks before going out means that you can leave the potty at home.

What You Can Expect

If you've ticked all of the above points then your son is very likely to remain dry on most trips out. There are bound to be a few accidents over the coming weeks, so take spare pants, trousers, socks, wipes and a plastic bag just in case. You can use a travel changing mat to protect your buggy seat.

How You Can Help Your Son

Make your first trip out quite short – about an hour. Long car journeys aren't the best way to start. A short excursion will keep you more relaxed as the chances of an accident are minimised. You can try going somewhere with a toilet – a local café or park perhaps – but you'll probably find that your son won't even need to go to the toilet on his first trip. However, when you get home do still give him lots of praise for going out with his big boy pants.

The Exception

Some little boys will suddenly insist on leaving their nappies at home even if they can't yet meet the above criteria and anticipate when they will wee and poo, or aren't yet confident about sitting on a toilet. But they love their big boy pants so much that they don't want to leave them behind when they go out. If this happens, follow your son's lead even if you think he's not quite ready. It's important that your son feels in control of his potty training and that you avoid confrontation. If he has an accident while you are out, don't make too much fuss; simply suggest that he wears a nappy the next time you go out.

Having said that, if you're going to be out all day, using public transport or taking him in the car, then this is where pull-up nappies come into their own. Just call them 'going out pants' and your son should be happy. And he may even surprise you by asking to go to the loo and keeping his nappy dry.

FIFTH AND FOLLOWING WEEKS – MORE TRIPS OUT AND BOTTOM WIPING

Although many mums would agree that potty training boys can be trickier than teaching girls, when it comes to leaving the house, boys are definitely easier. For a start, they can wee pretty much anywhere – just find them a patch of grass, a tree that 'needs watering' or a drain to aim down and they've got an instant toilet. Very often weeing outside is much nicer than using a dirty public toilet, and don't worry at all about any potentially odd reactions from passers-by – most people have absolutely no problem with a toddler having a wee in public so long as it's reasonably discreet.

On your early trips out, you can tell your son, 'If you need a wee you could perhaps water that tree/bit of grass,' as a way of reminding him to go and also showing him that you don't have to find a toilet – he'll be more open to this idea if he's had some practice weeing in the garden, if you have one.

Get him used to using public toilets as well as going outside. Wipe the seat first with antibacterial wipes as he's bound to touch it, and let him stand on your feet to help him be tall enough to wee into the toilet. Make sure you've got tissues in your pockets in case there's no loo paper, and carry an antibacterial hand gel with you so that you can wash hands if there's no soap available.

It's likely to take your son a few outings before he actually goes to the toilet while you're out, so don't worry when it seems as though it will never happen. Once it does, you'll both be much more confident about future excursions and feel happy to go out for longer. When this happens, you'll find that your little boy is pretty much out of nappies all day long, just wearing one for his nap and at bedtime (*see Chapter 8*).

The Dreaded 'I Need a Poo Poo'

This is bound to happen sooner or later when you're out. The best solution is to find a nearby toilet that's nice and clean. But realistically, chances are you won't be near one.

If you're in the middle of, say, a wood or common with no loo available, your easiest option is to quickly put a nappy on your little boy and explain to him it's an emergency nappy because there's no toilet nearby – this is also a good solution for public transport with no loos.

Alternatively, if you're outdoors you could persuade your little boy to poo on the ground then clean up afterwards, as you would a dog. So have some wipes and a nappy bag to hand. Some people carry a portable potty for just such an occasion.

Accidents When You're Out

Wees

One great thing about little boys is that many of them really don't care about being wet. This can buy you valuable time before you have to change your son's clothes – a huge relief if you've just reached the supermarket checkout with a trolley-load of shopping. But this doesn't apply to all boys so be prepared to rush off and change your son out of his soggy clothes in the nearest toilet or private corner.

Poos

This is about as bad as it gets. All we can suggest is that you find a baby changing room quickly and bundle up his clothes to be sorted out when you get home, then use wipes just as though you're changing a nappy.

If there's no toilet or changing facilities nearby, find a quiet spot and again bundle his soiled clothes into a bag, and use wipes. Speed, not perfection, is the best way out of this predicament. You can do a proper job when you get home.

It's essential that you don't scold or react too strongly as this will not only upset your son, but could even encourage him to do it again. After all, if you're out and he's not getting enough attention, and then discovers that pooing in his pants gets him masses of 'mummy fuss', you'll have a real battle on your hands.

So keep your reaction low-key and try something along the lines of, 'Oh dear, you've done a poo in your big boy pants, but next time you can do a poo in a grown-ups' toilet when we're out.' And try to leave it at that.

Bottom Wiping

This is one of the final stages of toilet training. It is especially tricky for young children to master because they aren't developmentally able to wipe their bottoms properly until at least four years old. Younger than this, your son won't have the dexterity to do a thorough job. Also, his arms are still relatively short compared with his body, making it difficult to reach his bottom.

However, he is at an advantage compared with little girls because at least he won't risk giving himself a urinary tract infection if he makes a bad job of wiping his bottom. All the same, it's worth checking his bottom when he gets home from nursery (nursery teachers generally don't wipe bottoms).

Because he won't get help wiping his bottom at school or pre-school, it's important to teach him the basics, even if he can't yet do a good job. We suggest that you start teaching your little boy how to wipe his bottom from the age of about three onwards. Wait until your son is able to reliably announce that he needs a poo, then suggest that he goes to the toilet by himself and you'll be up in a few minutes to wipe his bottom. This is the first step to independence.

The next step is to show him how he can hold the toilet paper to cover his fingers to avoid getting poo on them, and how to bend his arm round to reach his bottom. This requires a lot of dexterity and your son will definitely find it less of a struggle over the coming months as he grows and his arms get longer. As always, give him lots of praise, however messy his early attempts are – 'That's very clever, now Mummy will just do the final wipe for you.'

Good hand washing is now more important then ever and should have become a habit. You can always add a bit of interest by buying a scrubbing brush for his nails and a pump-style soap dispenser.

After the age of about four, some little boys can become reluctant to learn how to wipe their bottoms as they relish the attention from Mum and enjoy being babied. So try to teach him while he's still keen to be a big boy.

PROGRESS – WHAT YOU CAN EXPECT

It may take only a few weeks for your son to learn to ask for a wee or poo and to feel happy using the toilet. But it will probably be a few months before you never have to remind him to go to the toilet and he always goes by himself.

Bear in mind that it's normal to have the occasional accident between the ages of three and four, especially if he's engrossed in a game or playing with a new toy. This can explain why many little boys have accidents outside the home as life is more interesting and distracting. As always, keep your reaction low-key and never scold.

You'll probably find that you drop the potty-training star chart after a few weeks once your son has reached the stage where he no longer needs much reminding to go to the toilet and manages to use the toilet successfully most of the time. But you can always reintroduce a chart if your son needs any extra encouragement – say with hand washing, or perhaps going to the toilet by himself. If you have used a star chart before, make the new chart a sticker chart so that the reward system seems different. This way your son won't think he's regressed, but will hopefully respond with enthusiasm.

7

When Your Son Doesn't Fit the 'Mould'

We all know how different boys can be. And it doesn't necessarily have much to do with upbringing as two boys from the same family can be poles apart. One may be boisterous, full of energy and constantly in trouble for grabbing other kids' toys, whereas his brother may be easy-going, sensitive and even a little timid at times. So we've come up with some extra strategies to help customise our potty-training method so that it works for different children.

THE SLOW LEARNER

Some little boys can be very laid back. Although this makes them easy in many ways, as they generally have fewer tantrums and are very sweet natured, it can sometimes mean that they are slower to learn. You may find that when you try to teach your son to use the potty, he doesn't seem to grasp what he's supposed to be doing very quickly.

If this sounds like your little boy, then try getting him to teach 'teddy' how to use the toilet because teaching someone else a skill is a proven learning technique. Teddy can begin by wearing pants and using the potty, perhaps earning himself a gold star. Then your little boy could ask if teddy would like to try sitting on the toilet. What does teddy think about the toilet? Don't pick his favourite comfort teddy as this could get too emotional. Choose one he likes which happens to have legs that fit into 'big boy pants' and is machine washable.

Be sure that your son really is ready to begin potty training as there's a chance that he's not a slow learner at all, but simply needs another month or two to mature. So go through Chapter 1 in detail and check that he's both physically and mentally ready to come out of nappies. It's essential not to pressurise him or he could end up as a 'late starter' which takes longer to resolve.

THE LATE STARTER

Plenty of little boys still aren't out of nappies by the age of three, and if it seems as though potty training is never going to work, don't despair. What probably happened is that things got off to a bad start because you tried to teach your son too early, or perhaps you picked a time when he was going through a tricky tantrum phase. So you both ended up feeling like failures, your anxiety rubbed off on each other and now whenever you bring out the potty the two of you feel stressed and it all ends in tears.

But you can sort this out. Although your son is now almost certainly old enough to be physically capable of coming out of nappies, you need to give him a bit of a breather so that he will be mentally ready too. Put him back in nappies for six weeks and follow the early preparation tips in Chapter 2. Take care not to put any pressure on your son, so don't actually mention the potty in the bathroom unless your little boy does. And with our 'weeing in the cup' strategy (*see page 43*), hand him a cup when you put him in the bath and ask if he needs a wee – if he says no, simply say, 'Okay, maybe tomorrow.'

Don't allow yourself to put any more pressure on your son than this, however desperate you feel to get him trained. After six weeks, ask your son if he'd like to have a go at potty training and if he says no, continue with nappies for another week before asking again. It's important that you don't appear anxious if he tells you he's not yet ready. Just say, 'Okay, maybe next week.'

Once he agrees, follow our potty sessions training programme and your son will probably learn very quickly. The aim is to get your son's 'permission' to restart potty training as this will help him feel in control and less worried about the whole thing.

THE EASILY BORED CHILD

While most little boys will find potty training reasonably entertaining – after all, it's a new game and they get lots of attention – some will lose interest after a day or two. Such children are often very intelligent – the sort of boy who is extremely curious, always nosing through drawers and taking vacuum cleaners apart. If this is ringing bells then you'll also have discovered that your son is very difficult to 'train'.

A star chart just won't cut it after a couple of days, and the big boy pants and sitting on a potty will also seem a bit tedious. But we've found that bribery gets a very quick response. Explain to your son that he'll get a chocolate button or a couple of raisins every time he wees or poos in his potty. And assuming that you've picked a 'reward' that your son likes, you'll probably see results within hours. If so, it shows that your son was ready for potty training and also knew exactly what he was supposed to be doing but for some reason hadn't put his mind to it.

Bribery can also work well if you've had a few previous attempts at potty training only to discover that your son wasn't ready. If it's his second or third attempt then you may find that the novelty of big boy pants and star charts has worn thin, and a chocolate button can give things a kick start.

THE FRIGHTENED CHILD

For some reason, little boys can be more nervous than girls, and you may have found that your son seems frightened about potty training.

Fear of Pooing

Lots of boys get frightened about pooing and will refuse to poo in the potty. They would rather soil their pants than go in the potty. What's more likely to happen is that they simply wait until they've got a nappy on (usually at bedtime) before pooing.

If your son has issues with pooing then the best thing you can do is nothing – it's essential to stay relaxed or you could make things worse. This problem often resolves itself as your child becomes more competent about weeing in the potty and staying dry. But you can help things along by ensuring your child is eating enough fruit and vegetables and drinking plenty of water to make pooing easier because 'holding' poos can make them painful to pass.

Lots of mums have found that putting a nappy in the potty helps their sons get over their fear of pooing in the potty. But don't pressurise him if he's not interested. He'll get there in his own time.

Fear of the Toilet

The other big fear that many little boys have is of sitting on the toilet. It's very common for boys to feel frightened of sitting on the loo because they're terrified of falling down. But as we stressed in Chapter 3, child toilet seats can make the experience a lot less scary. So if you haven't already fitted one, do so before your son develops a toilet phobia, and ensure that it is fitted securely and doesn't wobble.

If you've already got a child toilet seat and your son still seems frightened of the toilet, then consider buying another model. Some are better designed than others – perhaps smaller and sturdier – so it pays to shop around.

Having a step to help your son climb on and off the toilet will certainly make him feel safer – being able to get down by himself will give him a sense of control, rather than being plonked on a seemingly high-up toilet and relying on someone to help him down again. So buy a step or stool if you haven't already, and check that it doesn't wobble and is a good height for your son to climb up, and also to rest his feet on when he's sitting on the loo – this will help him feel better balanced and secure.

Although we've suggested that your son learns to sit first because poos and wees can arrive together, if he seems particularly reluctant then it's worth suggesting that he stands up first. Just pick a time of day when he's not due for a poo. Use some of the tips mentioned in Chapter 5 to encourage target practice and make weeing down the toilet a fun game. This should help distract your little boy from any fears and familiarise him with using the toilet. The more contact he has with the toilet the more likely he is to try sitting on it.

Finally, some children hate being splashed when they poo in the toilet. But this is easily resolved by putting a few sheets of toilet paper down the loo first.

THE JEALOUS CHILD

There's nothing like a new baby to disrupt toilet training. Even if your child doesn't show obvious signs of jealousy he will still find having a new sibling very stressful and this will certainly affect potty training. This is why we advise not to start potty training when a new baby is due.

Regression

If your toddler is already potty trained, then it's common for him to regress and start having more accidents, both in the weeks before the baby is due and in the first couple of months after its arrival. This usually resolves itself after a few weeks if you're patient and play along with your child's regression. So if he wants to wear nappies again, let him. Likewise, allow him to regress from the toilet to the potty if that's what he chooses. You might think that your four-year-old looks ridiculous sitting on his potty, but just humour him as he's simply trying to be the much-loved baby again.

Deliberately Pooing in His Pants

Sometimes children can feel so jealous and frustrated by their baby brother or sister that they deliberately wee or poo in their pants as a way of getting attention. This is particularly likely while mum is breastfeeding and generally guarantees an instant reaction and a lot of attention – even if it is being yelled at.

Although a deliberate poo can be somewhat disgusting and shocking, it doesn't mean that your child is abnormal or is going to grow into a delinquent. It's normal and natural for little children to go to any lengths to get their parents' attention. The only way to deal with this is to minimise your response.

So, bite your tongue, put your baby in his or her Moses basket, clean up the mess while trying to stay calm and efficient, then carry on with feeding your infant. Only then give your toddler plenty of positive attention – perhaps telling him a story, singing together or doing anything that doesn't require your hands. You could even watch television together – don't feel guilty because coping with a new baby and a toddler means that you have to do whatever it takes to survive the early weeks. Just make sure that you watch his kids' programme with him and talk about it afterwards as this then counts as mummy giving him attention.

Do be prepared for a repeat performance at the next feed or at any time when you're giving your baby your full attention, but respond in the same way and this problem should be resolved within about a week.

8

Night Training

Stopping nappies at night can be quite stressful, and plenty of parents find this the most challenging step to the whole potty-training process. Like the first time you left your son without his nappy on during the day, leaving him nappy-free at night is a leap of faith – you cross your fingers and hope that he somehow crosses his legs until the morning.

One of the reasons that night training can be traumatic is that bedwetting means having to get up in the night, which has to be one of the most tedious aspects of parenting. Also, if your five-year-old son is still unable to remain dry at night you'll no doubt start wondering if there's something wrong with him, or indeed with you as a parent. But there's no point in worrying because children develop at different rates and it's normal for some not to be physically ready to go through the night before the age of six. In fact, one in six five-year-olds regularly wets the bed, according to the Enuresis Resource and Information Centre, and bedwetting is more common amongst boys than girls.

So if your little boy is slow to come out of night nappies there's nothing you can do to change this if he's not yet physically developed enough.

THE PHYSIOLOGY OF NIGHT CONTROL

For a child to be able to remain dry at night he needs to be physically ready. First, his nervous system must be mature enough to trigger a signal during sleep that his bladder is full and needs emptying. This signal needs to be stronger during sleep than when your child is awake, which is why children almost always learn to stay dry during the day before they can do so at night.

He also needs enough vasopressin, an anti-diuretic hormone, in order to suppress urination at night by slowing urine production. This hormone kicks in at any time between 18 months and about six years old.

Finally, the bladder must be big enough to hold a reasonable amount of urine. Bladders grow considerably between the ages of two and four, which is why many children start to go through the night once they are three years old.

A family history of bedwetting plays a large part in determining at what age your child will be physically capable of going through the night. So if your son is genetically predetermined to be incapable of staying dry through the night before he is six, there's nothing you can do apart from be patient.

Reassure

It's very common for children to need nappies at four years old and to wet the bed from time to time after that. But if it looks as though your son is going to have to remain in nappies until he's five or six, then do reassure him that this too is okay. You could even try explaining to him about brain signals and anti-diuretic hormones, and tell him that his body just isn't ready yet. It's important that you both accept this and don't try and battle against nature; otherwise he may end up feeling like a failure.

SIGNS THAT HE IS READY

Most children start to stay dry through the night a few months after they have learnt to be dry during the day – this is often between the ages of three and four. Some children will learn to go through the night at the same time as they are potty trained – by all means give this a go if you think that your son is physically ready.

But many children, particularly boys, take a lot longer to learn night control so you may have a bit of a wait.

Signs that He is Probably Ready to Try

- He stays dry during his daytime nap. This is one of the early signs that your son has some control over his bladder while he is asleep. So put a fresh nappy on at naptime and see if it's dry when he wakes. If he has 10 consecutive dry naps then you can try leaving the nappy off and you'll probably find he remains dry.

- He can 'hold on'. If your son is able to wait several minutes during the day between announcing that he needs a wee and actually doing it, then he has good bladder control and so will be more likely to be able to go through the night.

- He suggests leaving his nappy off at night. Some children are keen to be 'grown up' and will decide themselves when they are ready to go through the night. Sometimes they are over-optimistic and you may have a lot of accidents – but use towels and nappy mats to save on laundry and just go with it. If things get very inconvenient and he's wetting the bed more often than staying dry, you could always resort to pull-ups for a couple of months while he matures physically a bit more. Try calling them night pants, and explain to him that his bladder needs to get a bit bigger and this will happen soon.

Signs that He is Definitely Ready to Try

- His nappies are dry in the morning. This is the biggest giveaway that your son is ready to come out of night nappies because it's an indication that he has adequate levels of the hormone vasopressin, which suppresses night-time urination. If this happens most days for several weeks, then he is almost certainly ready.
- He asks to go for a wee at night. This is another sure sign that your little boy is ready to leave his nappies off at night because the signals that he needs to wee are now strong enough to wake him. Do note that most little boys don't ask to go for a night-time wee if they are wearing a nappy.

Night Poos

Although it's very rare for children to poo in the bed at night, your son might well poo in his night nappy soon after you've put it on following a day of wearing pants, or early in the morning. But as long as he's also happy to poo in his potty or the toilet, he's unlikely ever to poo in his bed once he's out of night nappies. So don't take late evening and early morning poos as a sign that he's not yet ready to progress.

STEPS TO COMING OUT OF NIGHT NAPPIES

Once you've decided that your son is ready, you can ask him if he'd like to leave his nappy off at night. If he seems happy about the idea then give it a try. However, if your son is reluctant to leave his nappy off at night, don't push. As always, minimise the pressure and simply ask him again in a week or two. A few accidents in the early days are normal, but if your little boy doesn't have more than four out of 10 dry nights our advice is to revert to night nappies for another month or two to give his body more time to mature.

Wait Until Your Son is in a Big Bed

Only stop using night nappies once your little boy is out of his cot so that if he needs to wee in the night he can easily get to the toilet or a potty by his bed. Ensure that there's a night light and a potty next to the bed, or that the hall and bathroom light are left on. Plenty of children get into the bad habit of having a night-time play session, so encourage him back to bed quickly if he does get up for a wee.

Protect the Bed with a Plastic Mattress Cover

You could also put a towel or a specially designed disposable nappy mat under his bottom for a few weeks as a precaution.

Minimise Night-time Drinks

Don't let him drink during the last hour before he goes to bed, but make up his fluid intake during the day. Allow a few days for your son's drinking pattern to adapt so that he is thirstier and drinks more during the day than at bedtime. Don't simply cut out night-time drinks because if your little boy gets dehydrated this can irritate the bladder and actually make him want to wee more frequently.

Get Him Up for a Wee

In the early days of night training this can certainly help avoid accidents. Children generally sleep for up to 12 hours, which is a long time to go without a wee, even by adult standards. But be sure that you wake your son up, otherwise you'll simply be allowing him to wee in his sleep; this could get him into bad habits and actually encourage bedwetting. Don't be shocked if your son has an erection as this is perfectly normal – just be sure to help him push his willy down when he wees to avoid any spills.

When to See Your GP

If, after the age of six, your son still wets the bed more than a couple of times a week, see your GP. You may be referred to a paediatrician who will rule out any medical causes, such as a bladder or kidney infection, then suggest ways to manage the problem. These include bladder training, bedwetting alarms (they go in the pants and cost about £30) and perhaps medication.

It's also important to see your GP if your son has been dry at night for a while – a couple of months or more – and then suddenly starts wetting the bed. This could be due to a kidney or bladder infection so should be checked out. It could also be due to stress, such as the first day of school, or simply because your child has started drinking more in the evenings.

Change the Bed Quickly if He Does Wee

Your son will inevitably wet the bed while he's learning to go through the night, and although it's a pain to have to get up and sort out bed linen, it's important that you remain calm. Have a clean pair of pyjama bottoms and a clean sheet to hand because you won't want to be rooting through linen drawers in the small hours of the morning. If you used a towel or nappy mat to protect your son's sheet, you may get away with simply removing these if the sheet underneath has remained dry.

Give Lots of Praise in the Morning

If your son does manage to stay dry through the night, give him lots of praise. But more importantly, don't get annoyed or worry if he doesn't. Wetting the bed isn't your son's fault and certainly doesn't mean that he's too lazy to get out of bed to wee. It's just a sign that he's not yet physically capable of going through the night.

9

Resolving Common Medical Problems

Although most potty-training problems can be resolved with patience and understanding, sometimes children struggle due to a medical condition. The following might affect potty training, and it's important that you seek medical advice if needs be.

CONSTIPATION

If you notice that your son's poos are dry and hard, and that he's straining quite a lot, this is a sign that he's a bit constipated. It's important to sort this out because painful pooing may result in your son with-holding his poos, thus making the problem worse. It may even cause anal fissures (*see page 125*).

In the long term, your son may develop chronic constipation when dry, hard stools become lodged in the back passage and watery poo from higher up the bowel leaks out. You may notice that his pants are smeared with poo even if you're sure that his bottom is being wiped thoroughly. Eventually, your son will start pooing his pants because the poo that is lodged in the rectum confuses the sensations in the bowel and he won't know when his bowel is full and he needs a poo. He may also become unable to tell when he needs a wee and start wetting himself.

What You Can Do

- Visit your GP who will confirm constipation by feeling your son's tummy, and rule out any rare anatomical problems. Your GP may prescribe stool softeners and laxatives.
- Ensure that he drinks plenty because dehydration can slow bowel movements.
- Gradually introduce more fibre into his diet by giving him more fruit, vegetables, dried fruit, beans, porridge and brown bread. It's important to increase his fibre intake very gradually because a sudden, large increase will probably cause wind, bloating, tummy ache and diarrhoea.
- Stress can make constipation worse, so reassure your son that it's not his fault if he's been pooing in his pants.

- Your son may have become anxious about going to the toilet if his poos have been dry, hard and painful. However, it's important that he doesn't hold on when he needs to go – poos can change from soft to hard and difficult to pass in a few hours. So get him to a toilet quickly when he says he needs a poo. Reassure him that pooing won't be so painful if he goes quickly and if he drinks plenty and eats the fibrous food you give him. Explaining to your son what constipation is and how you are tackling it will help him to feel less anxious.

ANAL FISSURE

Forcing out hard stools can cause small tears (fissures) in the anus which can make pooing very painful. This will make your son reluctant to poo, particularly in the potty, which will seem new and stressful if he's just started potty training. Instead, he's likely to want to go in his nappy because it feels safe and familiar.

There is often a bit of bleeding with anal fissures. This is nothing to worry about, once you've had the diagnosis of a fissure confirmed by your doctor.

What You Can Do

- Anal fissures are often a result of constipation (*see above*), so get this sorted out. Try not to let your son become constipated if he has an anal fissure because the combination of constipation and an anal fissure will be particularly painful.
- It's important that your son never strains when he goes to the toilet as this can cause anal fissures. A bit of pushing is fine but he shouldn't really force it as this means either that he's constipated or he should wait a little longer (another five minutes usually) before having a poo.
- See your GP who may prescribe a soothing cream to put on your son's perianal region – the area around the anus. Healing can take a while because the skin in the anus is wet.
- Use a small dab of Vaseline to lubricate the anus just before your son goes for a poo as this will help ease any discomfort.

URINARY TRACT INFECTION

If your son has been dry for a couple of months then starts having accidents during the day or wetting the bed, get him checked out because some medical conditions make you wee more frequently.

Urinary tract infections can cause frequent weeing. You may also notice that your son only does a little bit of wee at a time. With a urinary tract infection, there is sometimes pain on urination as well as a fever, vomiting and fishy-smelling urine.

What You Can Do

- Get him checked out quickly. Urinary tract infections are 10 times more common in girls than boys, and if your son shows symptoms it should ring alarm bells. This is because, being less prone to this condition, boys are more likely to have kidney problems rather than a straightforward bladder infection. The more quickly your son is put on antibiotics, the less likely it is that the infection will spread to the kidneys.

DIABETES

More than 1,500 children in Britain develop diabetes mellitus every year. This means that the amount of sugar in the blood is too high, and the excess glucose is passed out of the body in urine. So children with diabetes wee a lot more, and this makes them very thirsty. So if your son is weeing more during the day, seems thirsty, and is perhaps having more accidents and wetting the bed at night then get him checked, especially if he also seems generally unwell and lethargic.

What You Can Do

- See your doctor because diabetes must be managed with insulin injections. You will also be told about how to help balance your son's blood sugar levels by making sure he eats regularly and choosing particular foods.

TIGHT FORESKIN RESULTING IN RECURRENT BALANITIS

Lots of little boys have a tight foreskin. This is because the foreskin is attached to the penis at birth and gradually becomes free, so that by the age of four it can usually be pulled back. A tight foreskin can slow the urine stream, which means your son will take longer to wee. This can make potty training more tedious for your son so he may be reluctant to cooperate.

Sometimes a tight foreskin can result in recurrent

balanitis, an infection under the foreskin. This makes it very painful to wee, and the penis will become red and sore.

What You Can Do

- Take your son to the doctor because balanitis may need to be treated with antibiotics.
- Be very patient with your son when it comes to potty training and accept that it's going to take longer. If he's got balanitis he'll find it so painful to wee that he'll often cry just at the prospect of trying to wee in the potty. So he'll be less cooperative about potty training generally and may try to withhold his wee. Even in between bouts of balanitis he'll associate weeing with pain, which makes potty training more difficult.
- Talk to him about his balanitis and reassure him that you are aware it sometimes hurts him to wee. Then suggest that he only does potty-training sessions when it doesn't hurt – and let him decide. Tell him that he can always put his nappy back on if he changes his mind.
- Circumcision is often the best cure for balanitis. If your doctor suggests this do consider it very seriously. This is a common procedure, done under general anaesthetic.

HYPOSPADIUS

Hypospadius is a birth defect affecting around one in 250 boys where the opening of the penis is on the underside instead of at the end. This makes weeing standing up pretty much impossible, so boys with this condition have to sit down to wee. However, hypospadius is usually detected at birth and corrected surgically before the age of two.

What You Can Do

- See your GP to discuss an operation to correct hypospadius if your son hasn't had this yet. In the meantime don't attempt to teach your son to wee standing up; let him sit instead.

ADHD, AUTISM AND OTHER LEARNING DIFFICULTIES

Boys with any sort of learning difficulty will be particularly hard to train so you'll need plenty of patience. It's better to start them later because it would be particularly disruptive to have a 'false start' at potty training and have to restart a couple of months later when they are physically ready.

What You Can Do

- Follow our method. This should work well as it aims to minimise the pressure put on the child. Be prepared for potty training to take longer than for other children.
- Ask your GP or whoever helps you with your son's condition about getting some help with potty training. They may also give you some advice and tips that are relevant to teaching your son.

If your son's toilet training is delayed because of a medical condition then do be reassured that there is plenty of help available. And on those frustrating days when you think he'll never succeed, just remind yourself that he will get there in the end – and what's a few extra months anyway?

10

Moving Forwards

Once your little boy is asking to go to the toilet and having very few accidents, then by our definition he's potty trained. But this isn't the end – in fact it's just the beginning as he embarks on a journey of becoming more independent. Over the coming weeks and months he'll get more confident about going to the toilet by himself, washing his hands without help and eventually learning to wipe his own bottom.

The day he takes himself off to the toilet without even asking will be a very proud moment indeed as you witness your son making a huge step towards growing up. In learning to use the toilet, your son will have gained in self-confidence, and this will give him a huge head start as he goes to nursery and school and spends more time away from the home.

But once your son is potty trained, don't be surprised if he continues to have the occasional accident – it's incredibly common for children to wet themselves between the ages of three and four and even to poo in their pants sometimes. Most children won't have more than a couple of accidents a month and so are still 'potty trained'. And remember, nights don't count because staying dry at night relies on your son being physically mature enough, which is all down to nature.

We hope you've enjoyed our laid-back approach, and we want to leave you with a few final tips in dealing with some hiccups along the way.

WHEN YOUR SON HAS AN ACCIDENT

It's important to play down your reaction if your son should wet himself once he is out of nappies to avoid undermining his confidence. He will have come to associate using the toilet with being a big boy, so is likely to feel a bit embarrassed when he has an accident.

We suggest making light of it – 'Oh well, these things happen from time to time, you were probably too busy playing to remember to go to the toilet.' Or even using yourself as an example – 'Don't worry, even Mummy and Daddy had an accident now and again when they were little.'

DIARRHOEA

Toddlers often pick up tummy bugs, and a bout of diarrhoea is not unusual. We suggest putting your child back in nappies for a couple of days to avoid too much cleaning up, but do think about your son's dignity when you do this. Explain to him that he has diarrhoea which makes getting to the toilet in time extremely difficult, even for adults. Suggest that he wears a nappy just while he's ill and, as always, give him the choice. He'll probably agree, but if he doesn't, don't force him. Diarrhoea isn't usually severe for more than about 24 hours.

SETBACKS

Lots of parents have found that their perfectly potty-trained sons regress if anything stressful happens. This is particularly likely with the arrival of a new sibling, and when your son starts nursery or school. You may find that your son suddenly wants to use his potty even if he's been happily using the toilet for months. Or perhaps he asks to wear a nappy again, or simply has more accidents.

We suggest allowing him to regress to nappies or

using the potty if that's what he wants – just humour him and he'll soon get bored and start using the toilet again. Remember, he's only trying to be the much-loved baby, so do give him lots of affection.

As for having more accidents, this is partly due to wanting more attention, as we discussed in Chapter 7, and because he's more stressed he will also find it harder to focus on skills such as using the toilet. Again, keep your reaction low-key and wait for this to pass, usually after a few weeks.

Ten Signs that Your Son is Fully Potty Trained

1. The potty has become dusty and forgotten because he uses the toilet.

2. When at home, he takes himself off to the toilet without telling you.

3. It no longer occurs to you to pack spare pants when you go out.

4. You don't worry about car journeys and know that the car seat won't be wet when you arrive.

5. He can wipe his own bottom effectively.

6. He washes his hands without being reminded.

7. You don't think about getting him up for a wee in the night.

8. You don't pack spare pyjamas when you go away for the night.

9. When you're out he doesn't suddenly ask to wee or poo at awkward moments when there's no toilet available.

10. You never remind him to go to the toilet.

If you can tick 'yes' to three or more of these questions then congratulations – your son is toilet trained. And if this isn't the case, it means that your son is still learning so do keep giving him masses of encouragement – in a couple of months or so he'll be fully toilet trained and you'll finally be able to chuck the potty away.

INDEX